MOTHER, TELL ME YOUR STORY

♥

Mom, you mean the world to me. From the very first moment you cradled me in your arms, I've felt protected and safe. Looking up at your lovely face, I felt the unwavering power of your unconditional love and that feeling is the foundation of everything that I am.

You have always been there for me—for all of my triumphs and tragedies—offering a supportive hug, a boisterous cheer, a steadying pep talk or, always when I need it the most, a stern and honest appraisal. You're my rock and every day I strive to be a better person so that I might make you proud.

There are times when I feel like nobody could possibly know you better than I do. I can gauge your mood simply by seeing your eyes. I know immediately when something rubs you the wrong way and I can anticipate the very instant your face will light up with laughter. But now what I'm looking for is some deeper insight into how you grew to be the incredible woman you are today.

I want to understand as much as I can about the unique combination of experiences you encountered during your journey to now that went into making you, YOU. I want to know what you thought and how you felt, what you wore and who you were with during those formative moments that shaped you into the present day woman I admire and the mom I cherish with my entire heart and soul.

Please be honest, thoughtful and detailed in the answers you give to all the questions that lie herein. I hope you'll share everything with me: your funny stories and your sad ones, your great memories and most embarrassing moments. Nothing is too tiny or inconsequential, every detail is important to me as I truly want to know it all.

Mother, please, tell me your story.

CHAPTER I

EARLY CHILDHOOD & HERITAGE

A curtain fluttering in the breeze,

the reassuring smile of your favorite doll,

the sweet lilt of your mother's voice

singing you to sleep.

"A FAMILY CAN DEVELOP ONLY WITH A LOVING
WOMAN AS ITS CENTER." —Friedrich von Schlegel

What is your birthday and where were you born?

_____

_____

_____

_____

_____

_____

_____

_____

_____

_____

_____

_____

_____

_____

_____

_____

_____

_____

_____

_____

_____

_____

_____

_____

_____

_____

"TO GIVE BIRTH IS A FEARSOME THING; THERE IS NO HATING THE CHILD ONE HAS
BORNE EVEN WHEN INJURED BY IT." —Sophocles

What is your father's name, birthday, and where was he born?

What was your mother's relationship like with her parents?

_____

_____

_____

_____

_____

_____

_____

_____

_____

_____

_____

_____

_____

_____

_____

_____

_____

_____

_____

_____

_____

_____

_____

_____

_____

_____

_____

What was your father's relationship like with his parents?

_____
_____
_____
_____
_____
_____
_____
_____
_____
_____
_____
_____
_____
_____
_____
_____
_____
_____
_____
_____
_____
_____
_____
_____
_____
_____
_____

"WEEP NOT, MY WANTON, SMILE UPON MY KNEE, WHEN THOU ART OLD THERE'S
GRIEF ENOUGH FOR THEE. MOTHER'S WAG, PRETTY BOY,BFATHER'S SORROW,
FATHER'S JOY..." —Robert Greene

Do you have any siblings and, if so, please list their names, birthdays, and a short description of each.

_____

_____

_____

_____

_____

_____

_____

_____

_____

_____

_____

_____

_____

_____

_____

_____

_____

_____

_____

_____

_____

_____

"THIS IS THE REASON WHY MOTHERS ARE MORE DEVOTED TO THEIR CHILDREN THAN FATHERS: IT IS THAT THEY SUFFER MORE IN GIVING THEM BIRTH AND ARE MORE CERTAIN THEY THEY ARE THEIR OWN." —Aristotle

How did your parents meet?

Write down everything you know about the type of job your father had and the type of job his father had.

Describe your father. What were his hobbies?

_____
_____
_____
_____
_____
_____
_____
_____
_____
_____
_____
_____
_____
_____
_____
_____
_____
_____
_____
_____
_____
_____
_____
_____
_____
_____
_____

"NO MOTHER WORTHY OF THE NAME EVER GAVE HERSELF THOROUGHLY FOR HER
CHILD WHO DID NOT FEEL THAT, AFTER ALL, SHE REAPED WHAT
SHE HAD SOWN." —Henry Ward Beecher

Describe your mother. Did she work? What did she enjoy doing in her free time?

_____

_____

_____

_____

_____

_____

_____

_____

_____

_____

_____

_____

_____

_____

_____

_____

_____

_____

_____

_____

_____

_____

_____

_____

"MOTHER IS THE NAME FOR GOD IN THE LIPS AND HEARTS
OF CHILDREN." —William Makepeace Thackeray

Aside from your mother and father, what relatives do you remember being around a lot when you were a small child and what do you remember about them?

What is the very earliest memory you have? Describe it in as much detail as possible.

What details do you remember about the ritual of bedtime and are there any specific books or songs you remember your parents reading to you and singing to you?

"THERE IS ONLY ONE PRETTY CHILD IN THE WORLD, AND EVERY MOTHER HAS IT." —Chinese proverb

What stories did your parents tell you about when you were an infant?

_____

_____

_____

_____

_____

_____

_____

_____

_____

_____

_____

_____

_____

_____

_____

_____

_____

_____

_____

_____

_____

_____

_____

_____

_____

"WHEN PAIN IS OVER, THE REMEMBRANCE OF IT OFTEN
BECOMES A PLEASURE." —Jane Austen

What did your parents tell you about your first haircut? Who gave it to you?

What details do you remember about bath time when you were very young?

Describe the sight, feel and smell of a blanket you remember from
your childhood.

_____

_____

_____

_____

_____

_____

_____

_____

_____

_____

_____

_____

_____

_____

_____

_____

_____

_____

_____

_____

_____

_____

_____

_____

_____

_____

"WOMEN KNOW THE WAY TO REAR UP CHILDREN (TO BE JUST). THEY KNOW A
SIMPLE, MERRY, TENDER KNACK OF TYING SASHES, FITTING BABY-SHOES, AND
STRINGING PRETTY WORDS THAT MAKE NO SENSE. AND KISSING FULL
SENSE INTO EMPTY WORDS." —Elizabeth Barrett Browning

What did you name the first doll you remember having and what did it look like?

_____
_____
_____
_____
_____
_____
_____
_____
_____
_____
_____
_____
_____
_____
_____
_____
_____
_____
_____
_____
_____
_____
_____
_____
_____
_____

"ONLY MOTHERS CAN THINK OF THE FUTURE—BECAUSE THEY GIVE BIRTH TO IT IN THEIR CHILDREN." —Maxim Gorky

What are some stories your parents have shared with you about when you were a tiny baby?

_____

_____

_____

_____

_____

_____

_____

_____

_____

_____

_____

_____

_____

_____

_____

_____

_____

_____

_____

_____

_____

_____

_____

_____

What are some sensory impressions such as colors, sounds, smells, textures, or tastes that you associate with your very early childhood?

"MOTHERHOOD: ALL LOVE BEGINS AND ENDS THERE." —Robert Browning

CHAPTER II

CHILDHOOD

The smell of cookies cooling in the kitchen, the
feel of sunshine on your skin, the sound of a
page turning in a picture book.

"A MOTHER IS ONE TO WHOM YOU HURRY
WHEN YOU ARE TROUBLED." —Emily Dickinson

When you were little, what did you dream of being when you grew up and who encouraged you to believe it was possible?

Describe your childhood kitchen using all five senses.

_____
_____
_____
_____
_____
_____
_____
_____
_____
_____
_____
_____
_____
_____
_____
_____
_____
_____
_____
_____
_____
_____
_____
_____
_____
_____
_____

"A MOTHER UNDERSTANDS WHAT A CHILD DOES NOT SAY." —Jewish proverb

What were you were afraid of when you were little and why?

_____

_____

_____

_____

_____

_____

_____

_____

_____

_____

_____

_____

_____

_____

_____

_____

_____

_____

_____

_____

_____

_____

_____

"THE CLOCKS WERE STRIKING MIDNIGHT AND THE ROOMS WERE VERY STILL
AS A FIGURE GLIDED QUIETLY FROM BED TO BED, SMOOTHING A COVERLID HERE,
SETTLING A PILLOW THERE, AND PAUSING TO LOOK LONG AND TENDERLY
AT EACH UNCONSCIOUS FACE, TO KISS EACH WITH LIPS THAT MUTELY
BLESSED, AND TO PRAY THE FERVENT PRAYERS WHICH ONLY
MOTHERS UTTER." —Louisa May Aslcott

At what age did you lose your first tooth? What did the tooth fairy bring you?

Were there any pets in your home when you were growing up and if so, what are some details you remember about each one? If not, did any of your friends have pets?

How were you disciplined when you did something to upset your parents? What did you do to get in trouble?

"THERE IS NOTHING MORE CHARMING THAN TO SEE A MOTHER WITH A CHILD IN HER ARMS, AND NOTHING MORE VENERABLE THAN A MOTHER AMONG A NUMBER OF HER CHILDREN." —Johann Wolfgang von Goethe

What toys do you remember playing with when you were little and which ones were your favorite?

_____

_____

_____

_____

_____

_____

_____

_____

_____

_____

_____

_____

_____

_____

_____

_____

_____

_____

_____

_____

_____

_____

_____

_____

"THE MOTHER'S HEART IS THE CHILD'S SCHOOL-ROOM."
—Henry Ward Beecher

What nicknames did you have when you were little and were there any you did not like? Did any of them stick?

What type of clothes did you like to wear? Describe your
favorite outfit.

What type of games did you like to play when you had friends over?

"A MOTHER IS AS DIFFERENT FROM ANYTHING ELSE THAT GOD EVER THOUGHT OF, AS CAN POSSIBLY BE. SHE IS A DISTINCT AND INDIVIDUAL CREATION." —Henry Ward Beecher

Did you like to dress up for Halloween and, if so, what was your favorite costume and your favorite candy to get while Trick-or-Treating?

_____

_____

_____

_____

_____

_____

_____

_____

_____

_____

_____

_____

_____

_____

_____

_____

_____

_____

_____

_____

_____

_____

"OUR HEARTS GROW TENDER WITH CHILDHOOD MEMORIES AND LOVE OF KINDRED, AND WE ARE BETTER THROUGHOUT THE YEAR FOR HAVING, IN SPIRIT, BECOME A CHILD AGAIN AT CHRISTMASTIME." —Laura Ingalls Wilder

Describe the place where you spent most of your free time when you were little. Your room? Your backyard? A friend's house?

_____

_____

_____

_____

_____

_____

_____

_____

_____

_____

_____

_____

_____

_____

_____

_____

_____

_____

_____

_____

_____

_____

_____

_____

_____

_____

_____

_____

When did you learn to tie your shoes and who taught you? Describe your favorite pair of shoes from when you were little.

Who taught you how to swim and where did you learn?
If you never learned, why not?

"THE LOVE, RESPECT, AND CONFIDENCE OF MY CHILDREN WAS THE SWEETEST
REWARD I COULD RECEIVE FOR MY EFFORTS TO BE THE WOMAN I WOULD HAVE
THEM COPY." —Louisa May Alcott

When did you learn to ride a bike, jump rope, hula-hoop, or roller skate?
Who taught you?

_____

_____

_____

_____

_____

_____

_____

_____

_____

_____

_____

_____

_____

_____

_____

_____

_____

_____

_____

_____

_____

_____

_____

_____

_____

"A KISS FROM MY MOTHER MADE ME A PAINTER." —Benjamin West

What is an activity you used to do with your father? Describe your most vivid memory of enjoying that activity together.

What is an activity you used to do with your mother? Describe your most vivid memory of enjoying that activity together.

What are some of the first movies you remember seeing in a movie theater and who took you to see them?

"ONE MOTHER IS MORE VENERABLE THAN A THOUSAND
FATHERS." —The Manusmriti

Describe a memory you have of a sleepover at a friend's house.

_____

_____

_____

_____

_____

_____

_____

_____

_____

_____

_____

_____

_____

_____

_____

_____

_____

_____

_____

_____

_____

_____

_____

"NO LANGUAGE CAN EXPRESS THE POWER, AND BEAUTY, AND HEROISM,
AND MAJESTY OF A MOTHER'S LOVE. IT SHRINKS NOT WHERE MAN COWERS, AND
GROWS STRONGER WHERE MAN FAINTS, AND OVER WASTES
OF WORLDLY FORTUNES SENDS THE RADIANCE OF ITS QUENCHLESS
FIDELITY LIKE A STAR." —Edwin Hubbel Chapin

What are some memories you have from elementary school? Who were your best friends?

What are some TV shows you remember enjoying when you were little?

Describe some activities you loved to do during the summer.

What did you like most about school and why? What did you like least and why?

_____
_____
_____
_____
_____
_____
_____
_____
_____
_____
_____
_____
_____
_____
_____
_____
_____
_____
_____
_____
_____
_____
_____
_____
_____
_____
_____
_____

"THE BEST ACADEMY, A MOTHER'S KNEE." —James Russell Lowell

Describe everything you remember about your elementary school library.

CHAPTER III

TEENAGE YEARS

The wind in your hair as you ride a roller coaster, the
pulsing lights at a school dance, the nervous flutter in
your stomach when your crush grabs your hand.

"MY MOTHER HAD A GREAT DEAL OF TROUBLE WITH ME, BUT
I THINK SHE ENJOYED IT." —Mark Twain

When you were in high school, how did you imagine your future?

_____

_____

_____

_____

_____

_____

_____

_____

_____

_____

_____

_____

_____

_____

_____

_____

_____

_____

_____

_____

_____

_____

_____

_____

_____

_____

"A MOTHER ALONE KNOWS WHAT IT IS TO LOVE AND
BE HAPPY." —Adelbert von Chamisso

If someone asked you what is your greatest ambition in life when you were in high school, how would you have answered?

_____

_____

_____

_____

_____

_____

_____

_____

_____

_____

_____

_____

_____

_____

_____

_____

_____

_____

_____

_____

_____

_____

_____

_____

_____

_____

_____

_____

_____

What was your experience like as a teen in terms of fitting in and feeling accepted by your peers?

How old were you when you first started wearing make up? Who taught you how to apply it?

_____

_____

_____

_____

_____

_____

_____

_____

_____

_____

_____

_____

_____

_____

_____

_____

_____

_____

_____

_____

_____

_____

_____

_____

"HONOR THY FATHER AND THY MOTHER: THAT THY DAYS MAY BE LONG UPON THE LAND, WHICH THE LORD THY GOD GIVETH THEE." —Exodus 20:12

What is the first concert you ever attended and who went with you?

"EVERY BEETLE IS A GAZELLE IN THE EYES OF ITS MOTHER." —Moorish proverb

What is a cause you felt very passionate about when you were in high school and what did you do to champion it?

Describe everything you remember about your first crush.

What was the most embarrassing that that happened to you when you were a teenager and how long did it take for you to get over it?

_____

_____

_____

_____

_____

_____

_____

_____

_____

_____

_____

_____

_____

_____

_____

_____

_____

_____

_____

_____

_____

_____

_____

_____

"THE HEART OF A MOTHER IS A DEEP ABYSS AT THE BOTTOM OF WHICH YOU WILL ALWAYS FIND FORGIVENESS." —Honoré de Balzac

Describe the outfits you wore to both your high school proms and who took you. If you didn't go to either prom, describe what you did instead.

"AN OUNCE OF MOTHER-WIT IS WORTH A POUND
OF CLERGY." —Scottish proverb

What is something you got away with as a teenager that your parents never knew about?

How would your parents describe you as a teenager? Did you get into trouble often?

_____

_____

_____

_____

_____

_____

_____

_____

_____

_____

_____

_____

_____

_____

_____

_____

_____

_____

_____

_____

_____

_____

_____

_____

_____

_____

_____

_____

_____

How would your high school friends describe you?

"I SHALL NEVER FORGET MY MOTHER, FOR IT WAS SHE WHO PLANTED AND NURTURED THE FIRST SEEDS OF GOOD WITHIN ME. SHE OPENED MY HEART TO THE LASTING IMPRESSIONS OF NATURE; SHE AWAKENED MY UNDERSTANDING AND EXTENDED MY HORIZON AND HER PERCEPTS EXERTED AN EVERLASTING INFLUENCE UPON THE COURSE OF MY LIFE." —Immanuel Kant

How often did you get asked out in high school and where would you go on dates?

_____

_____

_____

_____

_____

_____

_____

_____

_____

_____

_____

_____

_____

_____

_____

_____

_____

_____

_____

_____

_____

_____

_____

_____

_____

_____

_____

_____

_____

"WHO IS IT THAT LOVES ME AND WILL LOVE ME FOREVER WITH AN AFFECTION WHICH NO CHANCE, NO MISERY, NO CRIME OF MINE CAN DO AWAY? IT IS YOU, MY MOTHER." —Thomas Carlyle

Did you have a curfew? What time was it? How often did you break it?

Describe a time in high school when you broke the rules.

Who were your biggest role models at this time in your life?

"WHAT DO GIRLS DO WHO HAVEN'T ANY MOTHERS TO HELP THEM THROUGH
THEIR TROUBLES?" —Louisa May Alcott

What were your favorite subjects in high school and why?

"LET FRANCE HAVE GOOD MOTHERS, AND SHE WILL HAVE
GOOD SONS." —Napoleon

What subjects did you like the least and why?

_____

_____

_____

_____

_____

_____

_____

_____

_____

_____

_____

_____

_____

_____

_____

_____

_____

_____

_____

_____

_____

_____

_____

_____

_____

_____

_____

_____

Describe your most influential teacher from high school and what class they taught.

Did you play sports? What sort of extra-curricular activities did you participate in?

"TOO MANY PARENTS MAKE LIFE HARD FOR THEIR CHILDREN BY TRYING, TOO ZEALOUSLY, TO MAKE IT EASY FOR THEM." —Johann Wolfgang von Goethe

What was your favorite type of music to listen to when you were a teenager? List 10 of your favorite bands or singers.

_____

_____

_____

_____

_____

_____

_____

_____

_____

_____

_____

_____

_____

_____

_____

_____

_____

_____

_____

_____

_____

_____

_____

_____

_____

"ALL THAT I AM, MY MOTHER MADE ME." —John Quincy Adams

What is something you achieved in high school that made you feel proud.

List the movies you remember best from your teen years. Did you have a favorite movie star?

Did you ever dye your hair or get a strange haircut?

_____

_____

_____

_____

_____

_____

_____

_____

_____

_____

_____

_____

_____

_____

_____

_____

_____

_____

_____

_____

_____

_____

_____

_____

_____

_____

_____

_____

"NATURE'S LOVING PROXY, THE WATCHFUL MOTHER." —Edward Bulwer-Lytton

Describe your bedroom in detail for me. Did you put posters on the walls or have special decorations?

_____

_____

_____

_____

_____

_____

_____

_____

_____

_____

_____

_____

_____

_____

_____

_____

_____

_____

_____

_____

_____

_____

_____

_____

_____

_____

"O PEOPLE, RESPECT THE WOMEN WHO HAVE BORN YOU." —The Koran

Describe a typical school night for you during high school, what did you do after your last class let out until bedtime?

Tell me about three people you personally knew who you admired as a teen.

Did you keep a diary or journal? What sorts of things did you write in it?

_____

_____

_____

_____

_____

_____

_____

_____

_____

_____

_____

_____

_____

_____

_____

_____

_____

_____

_____

_____

_____

_____

_____

_____

_____

"MOTHER'S LOVE IS EVER IN ITS SPRING." —Old proverb

Where did you hang out as a teenager? Did you go to the mall on weekends?

"EVERY MOTHER'S CHILD IS HANDSOME." —German proverb

How did you stay in touch with your friends in the years before social media? Did you talk a lot on the phone?

What sorts of things did you collect? Do you still have a collection from those days?

Describe your best friend from high school. Are you still friend with this person? When is the last time you were in contact?

_____

_____

_____

_____

_____

_____

_____

_____

_____

_____

_____

_____

_____

_____

_____

_____

_____

_____

_____

_____

_____

_____

_____

_____

_____

_____

"IF I WAS DAMNED OF BODY AND SOUL, I KNOW WHOSE PRAYERS WOULD MAKE ME WHOLE, MOTHER O' MINE, O MOTHER O'MINE." —Rudyard Kipling

Did you learn to cook in high school? List some of your favorite recipes.

_____

_____

_____

_____

_____

_____

_____

_____

_____

_____

_____

_____

_____

_____

_____

_____

_____

_____

_____

_____

_____

_____

_____

_____

"MAMA, THE MORE I KNOW OF THE WORLD, THE MORE I AM CONVINCED THAT I
SHALL NEVER SEE A MAN WHOM I CAN REALLY LOVE." —Jane Austen

Describe any summer jobs you had, or the chores you did around the house.

Tell me about what kind of clothes you liked. What did you wear on a typical day?

Describe what type of art you liked to make as a teenager. Paintings, photographs, collages, pottery, writing... what do you consider your masterpiece to be from that time?

_____
_____
_____
_____
_____
_____
_____
_____
_____
_____
_____
_____
_____
_____
_____
_____
_____
_____
_____
_____
_____
_____
_____
_____
_____

"BEFORE A DAY WAS OVER, HOME COMES THE ROVER, FOR MOTHER'S KISS— SWEETER THIS THAN ANY OTHER THING!" —William Allingham

Did you study a foreign language or know any foreign exchange students?

_____

_____

_____

_____

_____

_____

_____

_____

_____

_____

_____

_____

_____

_____

_____

_____

_____

_____

_____

_____

_____

"THERE NEVER WAS A WOMAN LIKE HER. SHE WAS GENTLE AS A DOVE AND BRAVE
AS A LIONESS... THE MEMORY OF MY MOTHER AND HER TEACHINGS WERE, AFTER
ALL, THE ONLY CAPITAL I HAD TO START LIFE WITH, AND ON THAT CAPITAL I HAVE
MADE MY WAY." —Andrew Jackson

Did you visit any other cities or countries when you were in high school?

Describe your perfect summer day when you were a teenager.

What do you miss the most about being a teenager and why?

_____

_____

_____

_____

_____

_____

_____

_____

_____

_____

_____

_____

_____

_____

_____

_____

_____

_____

_____

_____

_____

_____

_____

_____

_____

_____

_____

CHAPTER IV

YOUNG ADULTHOOD

The exhilaration of dancing with friends all night at a club, the thrill of tasting unfamiliar food in a foreign country, the warm glow of pride after your first promotion.

"GOD COULD NOT BE EVERYWHERE, AND THEREFORE HE MADE MOTHERS." —Rudyard Kipling

What was your first full-time job? Describe your responsibilities.

What motivated you when you were a young adult? What were some things you felt passionate about?

_____

_____

_____

_____

_____

_____

_____

_____

_____

_____

_____

_____

_____

_____

_____

_____

_____

_____

_____

_____

_____

_____

_____

_____

"ALL THAT I AM OR EVER HOPE TO BE, I OWE TO MY ANGEL
MOTHER." —Abraham Lincoln

Describe a really terrible date you suffered through as a young adult.

_____

_____

_____

_____

_____

_____

_____

_____

_____

_____

_____

_____

_____

_____

_____

_____

_____

_____

_____

_____

_____

_____

_____

"IN THE HEAVENS ABOVE, THE ANGELS, WHISPERING TO ONE ANOTHER, CAN
FIND, AMONG THEIR BURNING TERMS OF LOVE, NONE SO DEVOTIONAL AS THAT
OF 'MOTHER.'" —Edgar Allan Poe

What did you consider to be your dream job when you were in your twenties?
Did you ever manage to get it? Was it all that you had hoped?

Did you go to college? If so, where? If not, why not?

Describe one the most fun memories you have of hanging out with friends in your early twenties.

_____
_____
_____
_____
_____
_____
_____
_____
_____
_____
_____
_____
_____
_____
_____
_____
_____
_____
_____
_____
_____
_____
_____
_____
_____
_____

"A MAN MAY ACCOMPLISH IMPORTANT ENTERPRISES, HE MAY BECOME
FAMOUS, HE MAY WIN THE APPLAUSE OF HIS FELLOWS, HE MAY EVEN DO PUBLIC
SERVICE AND DESERVE A MEASURE OF POPULAR APPROVAL, BUT HE IS NOT
RIGHT AT HEART AND NEVER CAN BE TRULY GREAT IF HE FORGETS
HIS MOTHER." —Grover Cleveland

Describe the first place you lived outside of your parents' house. Who did you live with?

_____

_____

_____

_____

_____

_____

_____

_____

_____

_____

_____

_____

_____

_____

_____

_____

_____

_____

_____

_____

_____

"A MOTHER IS THE TRUEST FRIEND WE HAVE, WHEN TRIALS HEAVY AND SUDDEN, FALL UPON US; WHEN ADVERSITY TAKES THE PLACE OF PROSPERITY; WHEN FRIENDS WHO REJOICE WITH US IN OUR SUNSHINE DESERT US; WHEN TROUBLE THICKENS AROUND US, STILL WILL SHE CLING TO US, AND ENDEAVOR BY HER KIND PRECEPTS AND COUNSELS TO DISSIPATE THE CLOUDS OF DARKNESS, AND CAUSE PEACE TO RETURN TO OUR HEARTS." —Washington Irving

Name three big events, personal or otherwise, that shaped your life as a young adult and how they changed your outlook.

_____

_____

_____

_____

_____

_____

_____

_____

_____

_____

_____

_____

_____

_____

_____

_____

_____

_____

_____

_____

_____

_____

_____

_____

_____

_____

_____

_____

_____

Describe an outfit you wore during this period of your life when you wanted to feel powerful.

_____

_____

_____

_____

_____

_____

_____

_____

_____

_____

_____

_____

_____

_____

_____

_____

_____

_____

_____

_____

_____

_____

_____

_____

_____

_____

Describe a memory you have of a fun day at the beach. Who did you go with? What types of snacks did you bring?

_____
_____
_____
_____
_____
_____
_____
_____
_____
_____
_____
_____
_____
_____
_____
_____
_____
_____
_____
_____
_____
_____
_____
_____
_____
_____
_____

"A MAN'S WORK IS FROM SUN TO SUN, BUT A MOTHER'S WORK IS NEVER DONE." —Unknown

Which alcoholic drinks did you enjoy in your early adulthood?

If you chose not to drink alcohol, what inspired you to make that decision?

"I AM THE POET OF THE WOMAN THE SAME AS THE MAN, AND I SAY IT IS AS GREAT TO BE A WOMAN AS TO BE A MAN, AND I SAY THERE IS NOTHING GREATER THAN THE MOTHER OF A MAN." —Walt Whitman

What was your favorite way to exercise? Describe your fitness routine.

Describe the best date you ever had.

Tell me about the jewelry that you wore most often. Was there anything you only wore on special occasions?

_____

_____

_____

_____

_____

_____

_____

_____

_____

_____

_____

_____

_____

_____

_____

_____

_____

_____

_____

_____

_____

_____

_____

"THE MOTHER IS THE ONE SUPREME ASSET OF NATIONAL LIFE; SHE IS MORE
IMPORTANT BY FAR THAN THE SUCCESSFUL STATESMAN, OR BUSINESS MAN,
OR ARTIST, OR SCIENTIST." —Theodore Roosevelt

Did you ever pull an all-nighter? Describe what that was like.

"WHATEVER ELSE IS UNSURE IN THIS STINKING DUNGHILL OF A WORLD A MOTHER'S LOVE IS NOT." —James Joyce

Describe the wildest party you've ever been to and how you got home.

Were you ever part of someone's wedding? Whose wedding was it? Describe what you wore.

Describe the first piece of furniture you bought on your own. How long did you keep that item?

_____

_____

_____

_____

_____

_____

_____

_____

_____

_____

_____

_____

_____

_____

_____

_____

_____

_____

_____

_____

_____

_____

_____

_____

_____

"CAN MAN OR WOMAN CHOOSE DUTIES? NO MORE CAN THEY CHOOSE THEIR
BIRTHPLACE OR THEIR FATHER AND MOTHER." —George Eliot

If you could pick any place in the world to go with money being no object, where would you go and why?

_____
_____
_____
_____
_____
_____
_____
_____
_____
_____
_____
_____
_____
_____
_____
_____
_____
_____
_____
_____
_____
_____

"A MOTHER IS A MOTHER STILL—THE HOLIEST THING ALIVE."
—Samuel Taylor Coleridge

What type of music do you like to listen to when you want to feel motivated?
Name your top three motivational songs.

Describe your go-to outfit for a date when you were a young adult.

Who is someone you felt envious of and why?

"I ENVY YOU YOUR PEACE OF MIND, YOUR CLEAN CONSCIENCE, YOUR
UNPOLLUTED MEMORY. LITTLE GIRL, A MEMORY WITHOUT BLOT OF
CONTAMINATION MUST BE AN EXQUISITE TREASURE-AN INEXHAUSTIBLE SOURCE
OF PURE REFRESHMENT: IS IT NOT?" —Charlotte Brontë

When you were a young adult, what was your favorite way to unwind when you were stressed out?

_____

_____

_____

_____

_____

_____

_____

_____

_____

_____

_____

_____

_____

_____

_____

_____

_____

_____

_____

_____

_____

_____

_____

_____

"AS IS THE MOTHER, SO IS HER DAUGHTER." —Ezekiel 16:4

Who is someone you found intimidating and why?

What is the first thing people would notice about you if they met you at a party?

_____

_____

_____

_____

_____

_____

_____

_____

_____

_____

_____

_____

_____

_____

_____

_____

_____

_____

_____

_____

_____

_____

_____

_____

_____

_____

_____

_____

Describe something you've done that was really reckless.

_____

_____

_____

_____

_____

_____

_____

_____

_____

_____

_____

_____

_____

_____

_____

_____

_____

_____

_____

_____

_____

_____

_____

_____

_____

"A MOTHER IS YOUR FIRST FRIEND, YOUR BEST FRIEND, YOUR
FOREVER FRIEND." —Unknown

Did you like to sing? Have you ever sung in the shower? What songs? What's your karaoke go-to?

_____

_____

_____

_____

_____

_____

_____

_____

_____

_____

_____

_____

_____

_____

_____

_____

_____

_____

_____

_____

_____

_____

_____

_____

"AUTHORITY IS JUST AND FAITHFUL IN ALL MATTERS OF PROMISE-KEEPING; IT IS
ALSO CONSIDERATE, AND THAT IS WHY A GOOD MOTHER IS
THE BEST HOME-RULER." —Charlotte Mason

If I asked your best friend from this time of your life to describe you, what would they say?

What are eight things that you always carried with you?

What was your sense of purpose? What motivated you to get up in the morning?

_____
_____
_____
_____
_____
_____
_____
_____
_____
_____
_____
_____
_____
_____
_____
_____
_____
_____
_____
_____
_____
_____
_____
_____
_____
_____
_____

"ART IS THE CHILD OF NATURE IN WHOM WE TRACE THE FEATURES OF THE MOTHERS FACE." —Henry Wadsworth Longfellow

What were three of your most treasured possessions from this time in your life and do you still have them?

_____

_____

_____

_____

_____

_____

_____

_____

_____

_____

_____

_____

_____

_____

_____

_____

_____

_____

_____

_____

_____

_____

_____

_____

_____

_____

"THOU ART THY MOTHER'S GLASS, AND SHE IN THEE CALLS BACK THE LOVELY APRIL OF HER PRIME..." —William Shakespeare

What were some major things happening in the world that had an impact on your life as a young adult?

What was your favorite thing to do to pick up your spirits when you felt down?

How often did you see your parents or spend time with family during this period in your life?

_____

_____

_____

_____

_____

_____

_____

_____

_____

_____

_____

_____

_____

_____

_____

_____

_____

_____

_____

_____

_____

_____

_____

_____

_____

"PRIDE IS ONE OF THE SEVEN DEADLY SINS; BUT IT CANNOT BE THE PRIDE OF
A MOTHER IN HER CHILDREN, FOR THAT IS A COMPOUND OF TWO CARDINAL
VIRTUES—FAITH AND HOPE." —Charles Dickens

What is something you achieved when you were in your early twenties that made you feel proud? How did you celebrate?

_____

_____

_____

_____

_____

_____

_____

_____

_____

_____

_____

_____

_____

_____

_____

_____

_____

_____

_____

_____

_____

_____

_____

"A MOTHER'S ARMS ARE MADE OF TENDERNESS AND CHILDREN SLEEP
SOUNDLY IN THEM." —Victor Hugo

Describe the happiest day you can remember from when you were a young adult.

List your tattoos in the order in which you got them. If you don't have any tattoos, did you ever consider getting one? Of what?

What is your biggest pet peeve?

_____
_____
_____
_____
_____
_____
_____
_____
_____
_____
_____
_____
_____
_____
_____
_____
_____
_____
_____
_____
_____
_____
_____
_____
_____
_____
_____
_____

"A WOMAN'S LOVE IS MIGHTY, BUT A MOTHER'S HEART IS WEAK, AND BY ITS
WEAKNESS OVERCOMES." —James Russell Lowell

Describe a time when you went out of your way for a friend.

_____

_____

_____

_____

_____

_____

_____

_____

_____

_____

_____

_____

_____

_____

_____

_____

_____

_____

_____

_____

_____

_____

_____

_____

_____

_____

"GOVERN A FAMILY AS YOU WOULD COOK A SMALL FISH—
VERY GENTLY." —Chinese proverb

What do you miss the most about being in your twenties and why?

CHAPTER V

ADULTHOOD

The color of the sunset on your wedding day, the angelic expression on the face of your first child while napping, a cozy evening in with family while raindrops splash against the windows.

Using all five senses, describe your wedding day.

_____

_____

_____

_____

_____

_____

_____

_____

_____

_____

_____

_____

_____

_____

_____

_____

_____

_____

_____

_____

_____

_____

_____

_____

_____

_____

_____

"THE FUTURE OF SOCIETY IS IN THE HANDS OF THE MOTHERS. IF THE WORLD WAS
LOST THROUGH WOMAN, SHE ALONE CAN SAVE IT." —Louis de Beaufort

What are you most afraid of and what steps do you take to combat that fear?

Tell the story of how you met your spouse.

How were you proposed to? Were you surprised?

_____
_____
_____
_____
_____
_____
_____
_____
_____
_____
_____
_____
_____
_____
_____
_____
_____
_____
_____
_____
_____
_____
_____
_____
_____
_____

"WHO TAKES THE CHILD BY THE HAND TAKES THE MOTHER BY
THE HEART." —Danish proverb

Describe your ideal day of relaxation.

_____

_____

_____

_____

_____

_____

_____

_____

_____

_____

_____

_____

_____

_____

_____

_____

_____

_____

_____

_____

_____

_____

_____

_____

_____

"MY MOTHER HAD A SLENDER, SMALL BODY, BUT A LARGE HEART—A HEART SO
LARGE THAT EVERYBODY'S JOYS FOUND WELCOME IN IT, AND
HOSPITABLE ACCOMMODATION." —Mark Twain

What is a recurring dream you have and how often do you have it?

List all the cities in the United States that you've visited.

List all the countries in the world that you've visited.

_____
_____
_____
_____
_____
_____
_____
_____
_____
_____
_____
_____
_____
_____
_____
_____
_____
_____
_____
_____
_____
_____
_____
_____
_____
_____
_____
_____

"IN FAMILY LIFE, LOVE IS THE OIL THAT EASES FRICTION, THE CEMENT THAT BINDS
CLOSER TOGETHER, AND THE MUSIC THAT BRINGS
HARMONY." —Friedrich Nietzsche

What is your favorite way to blow off steam when you feel really upset about something?

_____

_____

_____

_____

_____

_____

_____

_____

_____

_____

_____

_____

_____

_____

_____

_____

_____

_____

_____

_____

_____

_____

"TO UNDERSTAND YOUR PARENTS' LOVE, YOU MUST RAISE CHILDREN
YOURSELF." —Chinese proverb

Using all five senses, describe what it felt like when you were a new mother.

What is a cause that you feel passionate about?

Name five things that you're good at doing.

_____

_____

_____

_____

_____

_____

_____

_____

_____

_____

_____

_____

_____

_____

_____

_____

_____

_____

_____

_____

_____

_____

_____

_____

_____

_____

_____

_____

_____

"IF I HAVE DONE ANYTHING IN LIFE WORTH ATTENTION, I FEEL SURE THAT I
INHERITED THE DISPOSITION FROM MY MOTHER." —Booker T. Washington

What are some of your guilty pleasures?

_____

_____

_____

_____

_____

_____

_____

_____

_____

_____

_____

_____

_____

_____

_____

_____

_____

_____

_____

_____

_____

_____

_____

_____

_____

_____

_____

_____

"CHILDREN ARE WHAT WE MAKE THEM." —French proverb

Describe the weirdest thing that has ever happened to you.

What are five of your favorite books, who wrote them and why do you like them?

Describe a time when you did something nice for someone anonymously and why you were inspired to act.

_____

_____

_____

_____

_____

_____

_____

_____

_____

_____

_____

_____

_____

_____

_____

_____

_____

_____

_____

_____

_____

_____

_____

_____

_____

"A FATHER MAY TURN HIS BACK ON HIS CHILD, BROTHERS AND SISTERS MAY
BECOME INVETERATE ENEMIES, HUSBANDS MAY DESERT THEIR WIVES,
WIVES THEIR HUSBANDS. BUT A MOTHER'S LOVE ENDURES THROUGH ALL."
—Washington Irving

Have you ever attended a high school or college reunion? Tell me what that was like.

_____

_____

_____

_____

_____

_____

_____

_____

_____

_____

_____

_____

_____

_____

_____

_____

_____

_____

_____

_____

_____

_____

_____

_____

_____

_____

_____

_____

"REMEMBER TONIGHT... FOR IT IS THE BEGINNING OF ALWAYS." —Dante

What is your favorite holiday and why?

Using all five senses, describe your favorite place to go when you want some time alone just to relax and think.

_____

_____

_____

_____

_____

_____

_____

_____

_____

_____

_____

_____

_____

_____

_____

_____

_____

_____

_____

_____

_____

_____

_____

_____

_____

_____

_____

What is the best gift you've ever received, who gave it to you, and for what occasion?

_____
_____
_____
_____
_____
_____
_____
_____
_____
_____
_____
_____
_____
_____
_____
_____
_____
_____
_____
_____
_____
_____
_____
_____
_____
_____

"I HAVE NOT WEPT THIS FORTY YEARS, BUT NOW MY MOTHER COMES AFRESH
INTO MY EYES." —John Dryden

Have you ever been hospitalized with an illness or injury? If so, what happened? If not, when was the last time you visited someone in the hospital and who was it?

_____

_____

_____

_____

_____

_____

_____

_____

_____

_____

_____

_____

_____

_____

_____

_____

_____

_____

_____

_____

_____

_____

_____

_____

"AND ALL MY MOTHER CAME INTO MINE EYES, AND GAVE ME UP TO TEARS."
—William Shakespeare

What are three of your biggest worries and why?

Tell me what you do when you can't sleep.

Describe a song, a movie, a book, or a piece of art that moves you to tears.

_____

_____

_____

_____

_____

_____

_____

_____

_____

_____

_____

_____

_____

_____

_____

_____

_____

_____

_____

_____

_____

_____

_____

_____

_____

_____

_____

_____

_____

_____

_____

_____

_____

"ALL WOMEN BECOME LIKE THEIR MOTHERS. THAT IS THEIR TRAGEDY. NO MAN
DOES. THAT'S HIS." —Oscar Wilde

Do you have a bucket list? Describe a few things you would still like to do, or places you would like to visit.

_____

_____

_____

_____

_____

_____

_____

_____

_____

_____

_____

_____

_____

_____

_____

_____

_____

_____

_____

_____

_____

_____

_____

_____

_____

"THE LOSS OF A MOTHER IS ALWAYS KEENLY FELT. SHE IS THE SWEET RALLYING-POINT FOR AFFECTION, OBEDIENCE, AND A THOUSAND TENDERNESSES. DREARY THE BLANK WHEN SHE IS WITHDRAWN!" —Alphonse de Lamartine

CHAPTER VI

WISDOM

The warm glow of inner strength, contented laughter
during a perfect afternoon, the sweet perfume
wafting from cut flowers in a vase on the table.

"MEMORY IS THE MOTHER OF ALL WISDOM." —Aeschylus

What do you consider to be your signature dish, what is the recipe, and where did you originally learn how to make it?

What was one moment in your life where you wish you had been bolder?

_____

_____

_____

_____

_____

_____

_____

_____

_____

_____

_____

_____

_____

_____

_____

_____

_____

_____

_____

_____

_____

_____

_____

_____

_____

_____

"MY MOTHER WAS THE MOST BEAUTIFUL WOMAN I EVER SAW. ALL I AM I OWE TO
MY MOTHER. I ATTRIBUTE ALL MY SUCCESS IN LIFE TO THE MORAL, INTELLECTUAL
AND PHYSICAL EDUCATION I RECEIVED FROM HER." —George Washington

If you had the opportunity to ask your grandmother five questions right now, what would you ask and why?

_____

_____

_____

_____

_____

_____

_____

_____

_____

_____

_____

_____

_____

_____

_____

_____

_____

_____

_____

_____

_____

_____

_____

_____

_____

_____

_____

_____

_____

"HOLD DEAR TO YOUR PARENTS FOR IT IS A SCARY AND CONFUSING WORLD WITHOUT THEM." —Emily Dickinson

What do you wish someone had told you before you had your first child?

Is there anything in your past that you deeply regret and, if so, what is it?

_____

_____

_____

_____

_____

_____

_____

_____

_____

_____

_____

_____

_____

_____

_____

_____

_____

_____

_____

_____

_____

_____

_____

_____

_____

_____

_____

_____

What are the top three best moments of your life thus far?

_____
_____
_____
_____
_____
_____
_____
_____
_____
_____
_____
_____
_____
_____
_____
_____
_____
_____
_____
_____
_____
_____
_____
_____
_____

"SOONER OR LATER WE ALL DISCOVER THAT THE IMPORTANT MOMENTS IN LIFE
ARE NOT THE ADVERTISED ONES, NOT THE BIRTHDAYS, THE GRADUATIONS, THE
WEDDINGS, NOT THE GREAT GOALS ACHIEVED. THE REAL MILESTONES ARE LESS
PREPOSSESSING. THEY COME TO THE DOOR OF MEMORY UNANNOUNCED, STRAY
DOGS THAT AMBLE IN, SNIFF AROUND A BIT AND SIMPLY NEVER LEAVE. OUR LIVES
ARE MEASURED BY THESE." —Susan B. Anthony

What advice would you give your eight-year-old self?

_____

_____

_____

_____

_____

_____

_____

_____

_____

_____

_____

_____

_____

_____

_____

_____

_____

_____

_____

_____

_____

_____

_____

"'IT'S A POOR SORT OF MEMORY THAT ONLY WORKS BACKWARDS,' SAYS THE
WHITE QUEEN TO ALICE." —Lewis Carroll

What do you consider to be your four best qualities?

What would your friends consider to be your four best qualities?

What four qualities do you value most in other people and why?

"YOUTH FADES; LOVE DROOPS; THE LEAVES OF FRIENDSHIP FALL; A MOTHER'S
SECRET HOPE OUTLIVES THEM ALL!." —Oliver Wendell Holmes

Who has been the most influential role model throughout your life and why?

_____

_____

_____

_____

_____

_____

_____

_____

_____

_____

_____

_____

_____

_____

_____

_____

_____

_____

_____

_____

_____

_____

_____

"MOTHER'S LOVE GROWS BY GIVING." —Charles Lamb

If you could go back in time and do one thing differently, what would it be and why?

Describe your perfect Sunday.

What do you consider to be your greatest achievement in your life so far?

"THE HEART, LIKE THE MIND, HAS A MEMORY.
AND IN IT ARE KEPT THE MOST PRECIOUS
KEEPSAKES." —Henry Wadsworth Longfellow

How would you explain what it feels like to be pregnant to someone who has never experienced it?

_____
_____
_____
_____
_____
_____
_____
_____
_____
_____
_____
_____
_____
_____
_____
_____
_____
_____
_____
_____
_____
_____
_____
_____
_____
_____

"THE LOVE YOU GAVE IN LIFE KEEPS PEOPLE ALIVE BEYOND THEIR TIME. ANYONE WHO WAS GIVEN LOVE WILL ALWAYS LIVE ON IN ANOTHER'S HEART." —Cicero

What has been one of your biggest disappointments and why?

Describe a moment when you felt pure joy.

List six of your favorite smells and the memories they evoke for you.

_____
_____
_____
_____
_____
_____
_____
_____
_____
_____
_____
_____
_____
_____
_____
_____
_____
_____
_____
_____
_____
_____
_____
_____
_____
_____
_____
_____
_____

"A MAN LOVES HIS SWEETHEART THE MOST, HIS WIFE THE BEST, BUT HIS MOTHER THE LONGEST." —Irish proverb

If you could pick anyone, alive or dead, to have dinner with, who would you choose and why? What would you talk about?

"LIFE BEGAN WITH WAKING UP AND LOVING MY
MOTHER'S FACE." —George Eliot

Where are five places in the world you've never been but would like to visit and what about those places is appealing to you?

If you could pick one day from your past to experience all over again, what would it be and why?

What advice would you give to your fifteen-year-old self?

"SWEATER, NOUN: GARMENT WORN BY CHILD WHEN ITS MOTHER IS
FEELING CHILLY." —Ambrose Bierce

Describe the most decadent meal you've ever had.

_____
_____
_____
_____
_____
_____
_____
_____
_____
_____
_____
_____
_____
_____
_____
_____
_____
_____
_____
_____
_____
_____
_____
_____
_____
_____
_____

"A MOTHER IS SHE WHO CAN TAKE THE PLACE OF ALL OTHERS BUT WHOSE PLACE
NO ONE ELSE CAN TAKE." —Gaspard Mermillod

If you were able to time travel and go back to witness any moment in history, what moment would you choose and why?

Describe the first time you remember ever seeing the ocean.

Describe the first time you remember ever being on an airplane. Where were you going?

_____

_____

_____

_____

_____

_____

_____

_____

_____

_____

_____

_____

_____

_____

_____

_____

_____

_____

_____

_____

_____

_____

_____

_____

_____

"AFTER A GOOD DINNER ONE CAN FORGIVE ANYBODY, EVEN ONE'S OWN RELATIONS." —Oscar Wilde

What is the craziest risk you've ever taken and how did it change your outlook on life?

_____

_____

_____

_____

_____

_____

_____

_____

_____

_____

_____

_____

_____

_____

_____

_____

_____

_____

_____

_____

_____

_____

_____

_____

"MOST MOTHERS ARE INSTINCTIVE PHILOSOPHERS." —Harriet Beecher Stowe

What are your five favorite movies and why? How many times have you seen each one?

If you could go back and apologize to anyone from your past, who would it be and why?

If you could change one thing in your life, what would it be?

_____

_____

_____

_____

_____

_____

_____

_____

_____

_____

_____

_____

_____

_____

_____

_____

_____

_____

_____

_____

_____

_____

_____

"THE REAL RELIGION OF THE WORLD COMES FROM WOMEN MUCH MORE THAN
FROM MEN – FROM MOTHERS MOST OF ALL, WHO CARRY THE KEY OF OUR SOULS
IN THEIR BOSOMS." —Oliver Wendell Holmes

Describe a moment in your life when you were at the top of your game and how that felt.

_____

_____

_____

_____

_____

_____

_____

_____

_____

_____

_____

_____

_____

_____

_____

_____

_____

_____

_____

_____

_____

_____

_____

_____

_____

"I AM SURE THAT IF THE MOTHERS OF VARIOUS NATIONS COULD MEET, THERE WOULD BE NO MORE WARS." —E. M. Forster

If you were given a million dollars right now to spend on anything you want, what would you spend it on and why?

What advice would you give to your twenty-five-year-old self?

If you had to choose one animal to be your spirit animal, what would you choose and why?

"TOUCH HAS A MEMORY." —John Keats

Is there anything you wish that you had spent more time doing when you were younger?

_____
_____
_____
_____
_____
_____
_____
_____
_____
_____
_____
_____
_____
_____
_____
_____
_____
_____
_____
_____
_____
_____
_____
_____
_____

"SHE WAS OF THE STUFF OF WHICH GREAT MEN'S MOTHERS ARE MADE. SHE WAS INDISPENSABLE TO HIGH GENERATION, HATED AT TEA PARTIES, FEARED IN SHOPS, AND LOVED AT CRISES." —Thomas Hardy